EXPLORING THE DEPTHS OF

GOD'S LOVE

BY

CHARLES F. STANLEY

THOMAS NELSON
Since 1798

Published in Nashville, Tennessee, by Thomas Nelson, Inc., and distributed in Canada by Word Communications, Ltd., Richmond, British Columbia.

G̸B

Editing, layout, and design by Gregory C. Benoit Publishing, Old Mystic, CT

Unless otherwise noted, Scripture quotations are from the New King James Version. © 1982 by Thomas Nelson, Inc. Used by permission. All rights reserved.

ISBN 9781418541149

Printed in the United States of America

09 10 11 12 13 RRD 5 4 3 2

Contents

God's Love Letter to Us

The Bible is God's love letter to mankind. You may never have thought of it in that way; many people tend to think of the Bible as a rule book or a story book. In reality, the Bible is a magnificent love letter in which God tells His children how He longs to care for them and bless them, forgive them and shower them with His mercy, and protect them from their enemies. His love letter describes how He wants them to live so that they might avoid the painful consequences of sin and describes His desire to guide them into ways of righteousness and ministry that will result in meaningful, fulfilling lives.

When we want to know about God's love, the first place that we should turn is our Bibles. The Bible is the foremost reference on this subject. It is the reference to which we must return continually to evaluate our definition of unconditional, divine love, and to learn better how to receive and pass on God's love to others.

As you work your way through this study guide, I encourage you to make notes in the margins of your Bible. It is far more important that you write God's insights in your Bible, which you are reading regularly, than to write in this book, although places are provided for you to make notes.

This book can be used by you alone or by several people in a small-group study. At various times, you will be asked to relate to the material in one of these four ways:

1. *What new insights have you gained?* Make notes about the insights that you have. You may want to record them in your Bible or in a sepa-

rate journal. As you reflect back over your insights, you are likely to see how God has moved in your life.

2. *Have you ever had a similar experience?* Each of us approaches the Bible from a unique background—our own particular set of relationships and experiences. Our experiences do not make the Bible true—the Word of God is truth regardless of our opinion about it. It is important, however, to share our experiences in order to see how God's truth can be applied to human lives.

3. *How do you feel about the material presented?* Emotional responses do not give validity to the Scriptures, nor should we trust our emotions as a gauge for our faith. In small-group Bible study, however, it is good for participants to express their emotions. The Holy Spirit often communicates with us through this unspoken language.

4. *In what way do you feel challenged to respond or to act?* God's Word may cause you to feel inspired or challenged to change something in your life. Take the challenge seriously and find ways of acting upon it. If God reveals to you a particular need that He wants *you* to address, take that as "marching orders" from God. God is expecting you to *do* something with the challenge that He has just given you.

Start and conclude your Bible study sessions in prayer. Ask God to give you spiritual eyes to see and spiritual ears to hear. As you conclude your study, ask the Lord to seal what you have learned so that you will never forget it. Ask Him to help you grow into the fullness of the stature of Christ Jesus.

Again, I caution you to keep the Bible at the center of your study. A genuine Bible study stays focused on God's Word and promotes a growing faith and a closer walk with the Holy Spirit in *each* person who participates.

LESSON 1

Our Need for Unconditional Love

───── ❧ **In This Lesson** ❧ ─────

LEARNING: DOES EVERYONE NEED TO BE LOVED?

GROWING: AM I NEEDY BECAUSE I DESIRE LOVE?

❧

Name any problem that plagues our world today, and I will point you toward an underlying emotional or spiritual need in the heart of man. Drug abuse, child abuse, spouse abuse, poverty, war, violence, crime—each of these situations is the result of a ripple effect that begins with an unmet need in the heart of one man, one woman, somewhere on this earth. The person reacts to circumstances which he believes are related to his unmet need, in a way that is unhealthy, ungodly, and ultimately unsatisfactory—perhaps with an outburst of angry words, a drink or the use of a drug to attempt to escape the need, a retaliatory measure, or grasping for material possessions in a hope of resolving the need. At that point, a trigger has been pulled. Another person is caused to feel pressure to respond to the needy person's behavior, and the problem expands and intensifies from person to person until an entire family, neighborhood, community, city, or nation is involved.

The basic condition of man's heart is *neediness*, and the foremost need that mankind faces is a need for unconditional love. At the foundation of all other needs we find a tremendous need to be affirmed by someone who will accept us for who we are. We long for someone to affirm our personality, our unique abilities and talents, and even our foibles and flaws. We long for someone to say to us, "I love you," without adding any "if you," "when you," or "so why don't you" statements. We have a deep ache to be appreciated for no reason other than the fact that we are alive and we are a child of God.

Only God can give us this unconditional love in unlimited quantities. Only God has the infinite capacity to love in this manner. All human beings will ultimately disappoint us or fail us in their love because they are *also* in need of unconditional love. We should never expect from another person what that person is incapable of giving to us—not because they wouldn't like to love us in this manner, but because they simply do not have the infinite capacity to love us fully all the time, in all situations, and regardless of what we do.

To love a person unconditionally is not necessarily to *like* everything that the person does or says. It is to love the person *in spite of* what he does or says! To love unconditionally means to help a person become who that person *can* be in Christ Jesus; to help the person reach his potential mentally, emotionally, and spiritually. To love unconditionally means to forgive a person freely and as often as necessary. To love unconditionally means to allow another person to express his opinions and feelings and to function fully in his ministry without hindrance. To love unconditionally means to want for another person what *God* wants for that person and to be sensitive always to God's timing and God's chosen methods for accomplishing His purposes in a person's life.

A Threefold Need for Love

Our need for love manifests itself in three very basic needs: a need for acceptance, a need to feel competent, and a need to feel worthy. Only God provides a means for us to be *fully* accepted and reconciled to Himself and to others. He provides this through His plan of forgiveness.

Only God provides a means for us to feel competent. His provision comes to us in the form of natural and spiritual gifts, which He bestows upon us as our Creator. Only God provides a means for us to feel worthy and needed. His provision comes in the person of the Holy Spirit, who guides us into the paths we are to walk and the work we are to do, who presents opportunities to manifest His forgiveness, and who reveals ways in which we are to employ our natural and spiritual gifts.

Only God has a means for *completely fulfilling* our need for love.

God Desires You as His Child

As you read through this book, you are going to encounter God's desire for you. The simple fact is this: God *longs* for you to be in relationship with Him. He wants you to become the person that He created you to be from the foundation of the world. He wants to see you living a fulfilling, satisfying, and meaningful life. His desire is that you live as His child, in the fullness of His blessings, mercy, and grace.

What is it today that you desire for yourself? Do you desire to *receive* God's love?

And the glory which You gave Me I have given them, that they may be one just as We are one: I in them, and You in Me; that they may be made perfect in one, and that the world may know that You have sent Me, and have loved them as You have loved Me.

—John 17:22–23

How does the Father love His Son, Jesus? What does it mean that He has loved you as He loved His Son?

How does your need for unconditional love manifest itself in your life?

≈ In which areas of your life do you feel unloved or unlovable?

≈ In what areas do you need to show more love to others?

❧ Have you struggled in the past with the fact that God loves you? Have you found yourself rejecting God's love or shielding yourself from it? Do you know why?

❧ How does it feel to be loved unconditionally? How does it feel to love another person in this manner?

❧ Today and Tomorrow ❧

TODAY: GOD IS THE SOURCE OF ALL MEANINGFUL LOVE, AND HIS LOVE IS FREELY AVAILABLE.

TOMORROW: I WILL ASK THE LORD TO TEACH ME MORE ABOUT HIS LOVE AND HIS CHARACTER.

8

Lesson 2

You are Loved

———— ☙ **In This Lesson** ☙ ————

Learning: What exactly is love?

Growing: How is God's love different from human love?

⟲∞⟳

The apostle Paul wrote to the Romans one of the most tender and awesome statements about God's love in all the Bible: "The love of God has been poured out in our hearts by the Holy Spirit who was given to us" (Rom. 5:5). *Poured out!* The love of God has not been measured to us in spoonful or even bucketful quantities. It has been extravagantly, generously, abundantly *poured out* in our hearts. God does not love us in a miserly, stingy way, but with infinite generosity. The Greek word that is translated "poured out" means flooded or overflowed. God's love flows freely and powerfully toward us, filling every aspect of our being and flooding over us in amounts too vast for us to contain.

This verse also tells us that God's love is expressed to us *by the Holy Spirit who was given to us*. The Holy Spirit is God's gift to all who believe in Christ Jesus and trust Him as their Savior and Lord. The love of God is a gift to us from the Holy Spirit. It is the Spirit who manifests God's love to us so that we can feel it, delight in it, be comforted by it, and relax in it.

Time and again throughout the Bible we find this word *gift*: God's love is a gift, the Holy Spirit is a gift, His forgiveness is a gift, His mercy is a gift, His kindness to us is a gift. God is always moving toward His people and generously giving Himself to them.

> Now hope does not disappoint, because the love of God has been poured out in our hearts by the Holy Spirit who was given to us. For when we were still without strength, in due time Christ died for the ungodly.
>
> —Romans 5:5–6

What proof do you have that God loves you completely?

Why is the Holy Spirit given to all Christians? What role does He play in God's love to you?

The Greatest Sign of God's Love

Christians have a symbol of God's love that is not heart-shaped, but cross-shaped. The symbol of the cross tells us that God so *loved* us that He sent Jesus to die in our place. He loved us to the extent that He would send His only begotten Son to die the cruel death of crucifixion so that we might not experience the consequences of our sins but experience forgiveness and life eternal. John 3:16 declares, "For God *so loved the world that He gave* His only begotten Son, that whoever believes in Him should not perish but have everlasting life" (emphasis added). If you ever have a doubt about God's love for you, look at the cross. It is there that God expressed the *fullness* of His love.

To the Jews, the cross was a stumbling block, a sign of weakness. To the Greeks, it was a sign of foolishness. But to all who believe in Jesus Christ, the cross is a sign of the power, wisdom, and love of God (1 Cor. 1:18). The cross tells us three important things about God's love:

- God loves sinners.

- God freely bestows His love on all who will receive it.

- God's love is without re-call.

God Loves Sinners

The first great message of the cross is that God loves *sinners*. At no place in the Bible will you find that God loves those who succeed on the strength of their own willpower and then turn to Him. At no place will you find that God loves only those who are of a certain heritage or those who possess a certain educational degree or type of talents or skills. At no place will you find that God loves only those who are members of a certain race, nation, economic standing, or denomination. God loves every person, and He loves us *while we are still sinners*. This means that nobody is beyond the reach of God's love—there's hope for *everybody*!

> For scarcely for a righteous man will one die; yet perhaps for a good man someone would even dare to die. But God demonstrates His own love toward us, in that while we were still sinners, Christ died for us.
>
> —Romans 5:7–8

❧ What is the difference between being willing to die for a "good man" and being willing to die for a sinner?

❧ In what ways is God's love far greater than any human love?

⁊ Have you ever struggled to earn God's love? What was the result?

⁊ God's Love is Freely Given ⁊

The second great message of the cross is that God's love is freely given to all who will receive it. Certainly the death of Jesus on the cross was the most expensive price ever paid on your behalf or my behalf. Nothing could possibly be more valuable than the blood of Jesus Christ. But that gift was given *freely*—of Jesus' own will—so that we might *freely* receive it simply by *believing* in Jesus as our Savior.

There are no lists of things we must do to receive God's gift of love. There are no prerequisites we must strive to meet in our own strength. God loves us while we are sinners and *freely* offers us His love. Our part is only to accept it, to believe and receive.

What good news this is! God's free gift of love and salvation means there is nothing we must do to earn God's love. Indeed, there is nothing we *can* do to earn God's love. God's only motivation for loving us and forgiving us is the motivation of His own heart. We cannot make God love us, and we cannot keep God from loving us!

This does not mean that all people automatically receive God's love, however. Receiving is an intentional act of our faith. It is not a *work* but an intentional desire and willingness on our part to receive what God offers. God does not bestow His presence, including His love, where He is not welcomed. He does not force Himself into a person's heart. He offers His love freely, and whenever the doors of our hearts are opened to Him, He enters fully. Jesus said, "Behold, I stand at the door and knock. If anyone hears My voice and opens the door, I will come in to him and dine with him, and he with Me" (Rev. 3:20). We only need to open the door of our hearts to Him to avail ourselves of His presence and love.

๛ Have you accepted Jesus as your Savior? If not, what is preventing you from doing so right now?

For by grace you have been saved through faith, and that not of yourselves; it is the gift of God, not of works, lest anyone should boast.

—Ephesians 2:8–9

๛ What sort of "works" have you attempted in the past in order to earn someone's love? In order to earn God's love?

☙ What is the role of faith in salvation? What is the role of faith in understanding God's unconditional love?

☙ God's Love is Without Re-Call ☜

God does not extend His love and then withdraw it. He does not give His love conditionally—on the basis of anything we do—and accordingly, He does not withdraw His love on the basis of anything we do. We cannot cause God to stop loving us.

God's love is constant and abiding. It does not change; it does not waver or vary according to anything we do or fail to do. Even when we sin, God loves us. Even when we reject God, He loves us. Even when we walk away from His plan and purpose for our lives, He loves us. There is *nothing* we can do to separate ourselves from His love.

> For I am persuaded that neither death nor life, nor angels nor principalities nor powers, nor things present nor things to come, nor height nor depth, nor any other created thing, shall be able to separate us from the love of God which is in Christ Jesus our Lord.
>
> —Romans 8:38–39

✹ What powers and forces and circumstances does Paul include in this list? What can separate you from God's love?

✹ What does it mean that God's love is "in Christ Jesus our Lord"? What is required for you to fully experience His love?

Experiencing God's Love

God's love is absolute. The sad fact is, however, that many people do not believe that God loves them because they do not "feel" His love. God's love is present and offered freely to them, but they don't know how to receive it in a way that is heartfelt and meaningful to them.

We must *seek* the Lord if we are to fully experience His love. The Bible tells us that if we truly seek the Lord we *will* find Him. If we truly seek to know Him and to experience His presence, we *will* know Him and experience His love. Jesus taught:

Ask, and it will be given to you; seek, and you will find; knock, and it will be opened to you. For everyone who asks receives, and he who seeks finds, and to him who knocks it will be opened ... If you then, being evil, know how to give good gifts to your children, how much more will your Father who is in heaven give good things to those who ask Him!

—Matthew 7:7–8, 11

❧ In practical terms, what does it mean to seek the Lord? Give examples of how this is done.

❧ Why does Jesus use the verbs *ask, seek,* and *knock*? What do those words suggest about the process of embracing God's love?

To seek the Lord means that we make our relationship with Him our priority and foremost desire. No matter what happens to us or around us, we choose to obey God, follow God, and have a daily and intimate relationship with God. To seek the Lord means to want the Lord in every aspect of your life, every moment of every day. It means to be in pursuit of the Lord: eager to talk to Him, listen to Him, and to consult Him at all times and in all situations. Those who truly seek the Lord ask the Holy Spirit to lead them and guide them daily. They ask the Lord to meet their needs in His way, according to His timing and methods, including their need to experience His love.

> O God, You are my God; Early will I seek You; My soul thirsts for You; My flesh longs for You in a dry and thirsty land where there is no water. So I have looked for You in the sanctuary, to see Your power and Your glory.
>
> —Psalm 63:1–2

What does it mean to look for God in the sanctuary? How might this be done in your own life?

෨ Why does David use the image of thirst to describe his need for God's love? Where does such a thirst come from?

෨ Seeking with Expectation ෨

Those who seek the Lord *expect* God to answer. They are on the alert always for God's answer. They read the Word expecting an answer. They listen to sermons, Christian teaching on-line, Christian radio and television programs, and Christian music with ears wide open to hear God's answers to their questions and their needs. Those who listen *expectantly* are listening with faith. They are the ones who will receive what they are hoping for.

> If any of you lacks wisdom, let him ask of God, who gives to all liberally and without reproach, and it will be given to him. But let him ask in faith, with no doubting, for he who doubts is like a wave of the sea driven and tossed by the wind. For let not that man suppose that he will receive anything from the Lord; he is a double-minded man, unstable in all his ways.
>
> —James 1:5–8

❧ What does wisdom have to do with experiencing God's love? How is wisdom obtained?

❧ Why is faith so important in this process? In what ways does a lack of faith make a person "unstable in all his ways"?

So many people do just about everything *but* seek the Lord in response to their need for God's love. They try to suppress their need for His love, claiming that it isn't important to them. Some try to deny that God loves them, claiming to be unlovable because of sin. Some strive to meet their need for unconditional love by turning to people rather than God, always to their eventual disappointment. And all the while, it is so simple to do the one thing that is required: *Seek the Lord!*

Turn to Him today and say, "Lord, I need to feel Your love in my heart and in my life. I need to *know* You and to feel Your presence with me." Spend time with the Lord, reading His Word and listening for Him to speak to you. Those who seek Him find Him, and those who find Him find that His loving arms are opened wide to them.

In this the love of God was manifested toward us, that God has sent His only begotten Son into the world, that we might live through Him. In this is love, not that we loved God, but that He loved us and sent His Son to be the propitiation for our sins.

—1 John 4:9–10

How is God's love fully demonstrated in Christ?

Why does John say that God's love is not defined by our love for Him? What does this teach you about God's love?

❧ Today and Tomorrow ☙

TODAY: GOD HAS PROVEN HIS IMMEASURABLE LOVE BY SENDING HIS SON TO DIE FOR ME WHEN I WAS STILL A SINNER.

TOMORROW: I WILL SPEND TIME THIS WEEK STUDYING THE SCRIPTURES TO LEARN MORE ABOUT HIS LOVE.

❧ Notes and Prayer Requests: ❧

LESSON 3

God's Desire to Be Reconciled to You

─────────── ❧ **In This Lesson** ❧ ───────────

LEARNING: HOW DOES MY SALVATION AFFECT GOD'S LOVE FOR ME?

GROWING: HOW DOES SIN AFFECT GOD'S LOVE FOR ME?

∽

In the last lesson, we pointed to the great truth of the cross: God loves us so much that He sent His only begotten Son to die on our behalf, so that we might never die as a result of our sin nature, but be transformed into a newness of life that is eternal. When we believe in Jesus Christ as our Savior, we are fully reconciled to God. Our sin nature is transformed, and we move from a state of being sinners to a state of being forgiven. Our reconciliation to God is total and complete.

What does it mean to be *reconciled*? The apostle Paul addressed this question in his letter to the Colossians. He opened his letter with a prayer for these believers in which he said:

> Giving thanks to the Father who has qualified us to be partakers of the inheritance of the saints in the light. He has delivered us from the power of darkness and conveyed us into the kingdom of the Son of His love, in whom we have redemption through His blood, the forgiveness of sins.
>
> —Colossians 1:12–14

Paul made it very clear that our forgiveness puts us into a different status, a different kingdom. He then went on to say about Jesus:

> It pleased the Father that in Him all the fullness should dwell, and by Him to reconcile all things to Himself, by Him, whether things on earth or things in heaven, having made peace through the blood of His cross. And you, who once were alienated and enemies in your mind by wicked works, yet now He has reconciled in the body of His flesh through death, to present you holy, and blameless, and above reproach in His sight—if indeed you continue in the faith, grounded and steadfast, and are not moved away from the hope of the gospel which you heard.
>
> —Colossians 1:19–23

What can we learn from these verses about reconciliation? These four lessons stand out:

1. Our salvation is complete.

2. Our salvation brings peace with God.

3. Our salvation makes us holy, blameless, and above reproach in God's sight.

4. We are to seek daily forgiveness for our sins as we follow Jesus our Lord.

Salvation is Complete

The apostle Paul states to the Colossians that their salvation is *complete*. That is what Paul means when he writes, "all the fullness should dwell" (v. 19). The fullness refers to our spiritual wholeness. Paul wrote a few verses later to the Colossians: "For in Him dwells all the fullness of the Godhead bodily; and you are complete in Him, who is the head of all principality and power" (Col. 2:9–10). We move from one state of being to another state of being. We are no longer in darkness, sin, shame, guilt, and condemnation. Rather, we live in light, righteousness, joy, and forgiveness. The transformation is total and complete. We are either in one state or the other.

From time to time, people have said to me that they are almost to the point of being saved fully, as if salvation comes by degrees or stages. That is not what the Bible teaches. The Bible teaches that when we receive Jesus into our lives, we are *fully* saved, *fully* reconciled to the Father, *fully* forgiven. There is no point at which you can still be subject to condemnation, which is total and eternal estrangement from God. Rather, you are subject to justification, which is a total alignment with God.

We are not the ones who bring about this reconciliation. God does this work in us. And what God does is always perfect, whole, and complete.

Most assuredly, I say to you, he who hears My word and believes in Him who sent Me has everlasting life, and shall not come into judgment, but has passed from death into life.

—John 5:24

🔊 What does it mean to pass from death into life? What is required to do this?

🔊 What did it cost Jesus to accomplish this transformation in you from death to life? How does this demonstrate that you can never move back into death?

Many people believe that God only loves their good works, their good nature, their "bright side." It is true that God hates sinful thoughts, words, and deeds, but it is equally true that God *loves* you always. He *loves* you regardless of what you do. He *rewards* you, however, according to what you do.

This distinction between love and reward is critical to understand. Conditional love grants love as a reward for good behavior. Unconditional love separates love from deeds. Unconditional love is bestowed because of who you *are* as God's creation. It is granted on the motivation of who God is, not on what you do.

God loves always. The rewards we receive, however, are directly linked to what we think, say, and do. It is as we keep God's commandments that we truly grow in our relationship with the Lord and can receive the fullness of God's rewards. Jesus said, "If anyone loves Me, he will keep My word" (John 14:23). Rewards are linked to behavior; God's love is not.

The fact of God's Word is that God loves you *completely* as His beloved child. God does not say, "I love this child a little, but I love that child a lot" or "I am fully reconciled to this aspect of My child's being, but not that aspect of his character or nature." God is *fully* reconciled to you in Christ Jesus, and He *fully* loves you.

> There is therefore now no condemnation to those who are in Christ Jesus, who do not walk according to the flesh, but according to the Spirit.
>
> —Romans 8:1

In practical terms, what does it mean to "walk according to the flesh"? To walk "according to the Spirit"?

27

❧ Which walk characterizes your own life?

Salvation Brings Peace with God

One of the great marks of reconciliation in all relationships is genuine spiritual peace. Certainly that is also one of the great words that we associate with those who have a *loving* relationship with others. When a person accepts Jesus as his Savior, he enters a profound state of peace with God.

Peace and fear do not coexist. Our peace with God means we no longer have any need to fear God or to fear the consequences of our old sin nature. We can stand before the Father with perfect peace, knowing that all of God's intentions toward us are for our eternal good.

> Therefore, having been justified by faith, we have peace with God through our Lord Jesus Christ.
>
> —Romans 5:1

🕮 What does it mean to be justified? How does your justification guarantee your peace with God?

🕮 What is the relationship between justification and sinful behavior? Why do Christians sometimes sin if we are also justified?

Salvation Changes Our Identity Before God

When we accept God's forgiveness, we have a new identity in Christ. The "old man" disappears; we are new creatures. The apostle Paul wrote to the Colossians that before the Lord we are now:

Holy. The word *holy* literally means "separate." We are no longer of the world; we are of God's kingdom. We are no longer subject to the devil but subject to Christ Jesus.

Blameless. There is nothing held against us; the slates of our lives have been wiped clean before God.

Above Reproach. There is nothing the devil can point to and say, "That warrants eternal death."

Peter wrote that Jesus "bore our sins in His own body on the tree, that we, having died to sins, might live for righteousness—by whose stripes you were healed" (1 Peter 2:24).

  In practical terms, what does it mean to die to sins? To live for righteousness?

  What did Jesus heal with His stripes?

What does the peace of our salvation have to do with experiencing God's love? It is very difficult to *feel* the love of a person in whose presence you are afraid. Peace with God closes the door to fear and opens the door to experiencing God's loving presence: "There is no fear in love; but perfect love casts out fear" (1 John 4:18).

We Are to Seek God's Forgiveness Daily

None of us walk in perfect holiness and righteousness all the days of our lives. We continue to make mistakes and to sin. Some of our daily sins are rooted in what we know we *should* have done but didn't do. Some of our daily sins are willful acts of rebellion. But these sins do not damage our salvation. (If you have any doubt about this, I encourage you to read the Bible study in this series titled *Understanding Eternal Security*.)

The damage is not to our salvation but to two other aspects of our walk with the Lord. The *degree of intimacy* that we experience with the Lord is damaged, and the *extent to which we are able to experience the blessings* of the Lord is damaged. Disobedience does not produce God's rewards. To the contrary, it can *keep* us from receiving God's blessings.

We certainly know this to be true in our relationships with family members and friends. A marriage might not be destroyed because of mistakes that one spouse makes or sins that one spouse commits against the other, but the free-flowing peaceful intimacy of the marriage is certainly going to be damaged. A friendship may not be destroyed because of one person's sins and errors, but feelings of closeness in the friendship are going to be affected.

The same is true for our relationship with our heavenly Father. Sin pollutes the atmosphere of the relationship. It creates a hindrance, an obstacle, to our feeling God's presence and power. It keeps us from feeling totally free in the Lord's presence. Sin produces an impulse in us to run and hide when we hear God's voice, just as it did in Adam and Eve (Gen. 3:8).

How can we keep our relationship with the Lord free of the taint of daily sins? By confessing our sins quickly! Our immediate confession of sin brings about an immediate forgiveness of sin: "If we confess our sins, He is faithful and just to forgive us our sins and to cleanse us from all unrighteousness" (1 John 1:9).

We are also wise to ask the Holy Spirit daily to direct our steps away from sin and toward God's plan and purpose for our lives. Jesus taught us to pray, "Do not lead us into temptation [in other words, lead us away from anything that will tempt us to sin], but deliver us from the evil one" (Matt. 6:13). We must strive to lead a life that is pure and holy before the Lord; we must never think that it is acceptable to the Lord for us to flirt with sin or to engage in "just a little sin" from time to time. The Lord calls us to a *perfect* life, which is a life of wholeness, free from sin's pull and sin's consequences. As we live a life of purity, forgiven of our daily sins, we experience the fullness of God's love.

If then you were raised with Christ, seek those things which are above, where Christ is, sitting at the right hand of God. Set your mind on things above, not on things on the earth. For you died, and your life is hidden with Christ in God.

—Colossians 3:1–3

❧ In practical terms, what does it mean to "set your mind on things above"?

❧ What does it mean that "your life is hidden with Christ in God"? What does Paul mean when he says "you died"?

❧ What effect does this death and life have on sin's influence over you?

Reconciliation and Acceptance

Our need to belong—to be accepted—is part of our great need for love. God has met that need through the Cross. The forgiveness of our sin through Christ Jesus makes us totally acceptable to God. He receives us fully as His sons, His heirs, His beloved children. We fully belong to God.

God's acceptance of you as His beloved child includes an open invitation for you to come boldly into His presence at all times. It is an invitation to experience genuine fellowship with Him. It is an invitation to receive the warm embrace of His love.

> For those who live according to the flesh set their minds on the things of the flesh, but those who live according to the Spirit, the things of the Spirit. For to be carnally minded is death, but to be spiritually minded is life and peace.
>
> —Romans 8:5–6

✎ What does it mean to "live according to the flesh"? "According to the Spirit"? Give practical examples of each.

What does it mean to be "carnally minded"? To be "spiritually minded"? How does one avoid a carnal mind and develop a spiritual mind?

─── Today and Tomorrow ───

Today: God continues to love me even when I sin, but sin can hinder my relationship with Him.

Tomorrow: I will be careful this week to confess my sins quickly.

Notes and Prayer Requests:

Lesson 4

God's Desire to Free You from Sin's Power

---------- ❧ **In This Lesson** ☙ ----------

LEARNING: WHAT DOES IT MEAN TO BE REDEEMED?

GROWING: IF I SIN, DOES THAT MEAN THAT I'M NOT SAVED?

The person who genuinely loves another person unconditionally wants the *best* for that person at all times, in all areas of life. That is how God loves us. He desires the very best for His beloved children, including a life that is totally free from sin's power.

One of the most potent words a person can ever learn is the word *redeemed*. This word runs from cover to cover in the Bible. In the Old Testament, the concept appears more than a hundred times: God's redemption plan for mankind is established, God clearly states that a redemption is required, and the foundation is prepared for that redemption plan to be implemented.

In the New Testament, God's redemption plan is put into effect: in Acts the plan is extended to the Gentiles; in the Epistles it is explained; and in the book of Revelation it is ultimately accomplished. The great song of Revelation 5:9–10 declares in homage to Jesus Christ:

You are worthy to take the scroll,
And to open its seals;
For You were slain,
And have redeemed us to God by Your blood
Out of every tribe and tongue and people and nation,
And have made us kings and priests to our God;
And we shall reign on the earth.

The apostle Paul wrote to the Ephesians about the redemptive power of Christ's shed blood:

> In Him we have redemption through His blood, the forgiveness of sins, according to the riches of His grace which He made to abound toward us in all wisdom and prudence, having made known to us the mystery of His will, according to His good pleasure which He purposed in Himself, that in the dispensation of the fullness of the times He might gather together in one all things in Christ, both which are in heaven and which are on earth—in Him.
>
> —Ephesians 1:7–10

What does "redemption" mean? What are its practical effects in your life?

◦ What is the "mystery of God's will"? What is God's overriding will for you?

The Price of Our Redemption

To redeem is to pay a price for a person or object. In the case of our redemption, the price was the shed blood of Jesus Christ on the cross. The blood of Jesus Christ was required for our redemption. *Only* the blood of Jesus Christ, the only begotten Son of God, sinless and pure, was sufficient to pay for our redemption.

◦ What price did Jesus pay for your redemption? What does that demonstrate about His love for you?

ৰ Why was Jesus' blood necessary to pay for your redemption? Why would nothing else suffice?

The Necessity and Purpose of Our Redemption

Since the moment when Adam sinned in the Garden of Eden, every person has been born with a sin nature. We all know that from our infancy we have done things we should not have done and have known more evil than we ever should have known. We have had a sin nature that could not be dominated by our will alone. Sin had dominion over us—we were sinners by nature and sinners by action.

God's holiness and absolute goodness are incompatible with sin. God does not associate with sin and can have no part in sin. Our sinful nature, therefore, alienated us from God and put us outside the boundaries of God's intimate presence.

In His love God continually called to man. And in sending His Son to this earth, He made a full provision for us to be drawn near to Him once again so we might enjoy the intimacy of His loving presence. As Paul wrote to the Ephesians, "Now in Christ Jesus you who once were far off have been brought near by the blood of Christ" (Eph. 2:13).

The purpose of our redemption was to spare us from the consequences of our sin: eternal separation from God our loving Father. Our redemption makes possible our eternal life. But not only that—our redemption also frees us from the destructive dominion that sin had over our lives. We are redeemed for eternity, and we are also redeemed so we might live victorious lives *right now*.

> The Lord redeems the soul of His servants, and none of those who trust in Him shall be condemned.

> —Psalm 34:22

∽ Have you accepted God's free gift of salvation? If so, what does that mean in the eternal perspective?

∽ What effect does your salvation have on your life today? If you will not be eternally condemned, what impact should that have on sinful behaviors in your life?

Living in Daily Redemption

If a person redeems an item from a pawnshop, he pays the fee for the item so he can walk away with it. In the Bible the word has two meanings: first, to pay a ransom, and second, to buy and bring out of a marketplace.

❧ A Ransom Paid for Our Release ❧

Ransoms are generally associated with kidnapping, and in the spiritual realm that is exactly what happened to man. He was kidnapped away from God by the enemy of our souls, enticed and trapped and held in bondage by Satan, the deceiver. The shed blood of Jesus Christ was required so that mankind might be freed from this bondage and restored to God.

Who pays a ransom for a kidnapped child? The one who dearly loves that child, his father. It was out of our heavenly Father's infinite love for us that He paid the ransom necessary to get us back into His embrace.

How is a ransom price set? The value of the kidnapped child is determined according to what the father is *capable of* and *willing to* pay. The devil set an extremely high ransom price for mankind. He knew that we were infinitely valuable to the Father and that He would be willing to pay the ultimate price for our return.

Our ransom means that we can be restored to intimacy with the Father. We are no longer held in captivity by the devil. We no longer belong to him. Rather, we are free from him, if we will only choose to be free and to walk away from the devil and walk toward our Father. The bonds that have held us have been broken. It is up to us to step out of those shackles and chains and move toward God, receiving and believing in the ransom paid by Jesus Christ.

⮞ No Longer Enslaved to Sin's Impulses ⮜

The second meaning of the word *redeem* is to "purchase from a market." In the New Testament this word refers specifically to a person's purchase from a *slave* market. Slavery was common in New Testament times, and to be a slave was no joking matter. There are those today who joke about sin: they think they are free when they are sinning and a "little sin" can be a lark. The truth is the exact opposite: sin enslaves. It tempts us and then takes dominion over us. It is a snare, alluring with enticing bait that traps us and from which there is no escape apart from God's help.

Before a person accepts Jesus as Savior, he lives under the dictates of the enemy and all of the fleshly desires that are under Satan's influence: "the lust of the flesh, the lust of the eyes, and the pride of life" (1 John 2:16). The sinner automatically gives in to these lusts and to pride. He never thinks twice about doing what feels good to his senses or what he feels is right in his own eyes. He lives for self, doing whatever he feels he must do to protect and promote "number one." There is no genuine concern for others or for God's commandments, absolutes, or standards of right living. The sinner may feel guilt and shame, but these feelings do not keep him from continuing to do what brings him momentary pleasure. In fact, his guilt and shame may *drive* him to do what brings momentary pleasure and an escape from feeling the guilt and shame.

Once a person accepts Jesus as Savior, those bonds of automatic impulse are broken. Suddenly the person who has been enslaved has a true *choice* about how he will think, speak, and behave. The Holy Spirit who dwells within him makes him very uncomfortable with self-promoting, self-preserving, self-pleasing choices. The Holy Spirit continually compels him to turn away from sin and from a love of the world and to turn toward the will and love of God.

Do not love the world or the things in the world. If anyone loves the world, the love of the Father is not in him. For all that is in the world—the lust of the flesh, the lust of the eyes, and the pride of life—is not of the Father but is of the world. And the world is passing away, and the lust of it; but he who does the will of God abides forever.

—1 John 2:15–17

❧ What does "love of the world" look like? Give practical examples.

❧ Give examples of each area of lust: lust of the flesh, lust of the eyes, pride of life.

❧ Why does John say that the love of God is not in the person who loves the world? Why are the two loves mutually exclusive?

Can a person live free from sin? Yes! John wrote:

> My little children, these things I write to you, so that you may not sin. And if anyone sins, we have an Advocate with the Father, Jesus Christ the righteous. And He Himself is the propitiation for our sins, and not for ours only but also for the whole world.
>
> —1 John 2:1–2

We can live in a continual state of abiding in the Lord so that we keep God's commandments and *choose* constantly—moment to moment, day to day—to live according to God's plan. The Holy Spirit enables us to do this. John wrote, "By this we know that we abide in Him, and He in us, because He has given us of His Spirit" (1 John 4:13).

John also wrote that the Spirit empowers us to withstand temptations from evil sources, including evil people:

You are of God, little children, and have overcome them, because He who is in you is greater than he who is in the world. They are of the world. Therefore they speak as of the world, and the world hears them. We are of God. He who knows God hears us; he who is not of God does not hear us. By this we know the spirit of truth and the spirit of error.

—1 John 4:4–6

The Holy Spirit imparts to us the knowledge of right and wrong, and He also empowers us to make choices for right! The believer has to *work* at making a bad choice and giving in to the lust of the flesh, the lust of the eyes, and the pride of life. He has to go against the grain of his new nature, consciously and willfully choosing to engage in sin. The more mature a believer becomes in Christ Jesus, the harder that person has to work at making an active choice for evil and the more miserable he is going to be as a result of his bad, willful choice.

The Holy Spirit moves within us constantly to call us away from sin and toward righteousness. The Holy Spirit builds a resistance into a believer against evil. The genuine believer's desire is to follow the Lord, and the genuine believer's conscience therefore becomes stronger and stronger the closer and longer he follows the Lord. The believer is simply no longer *enslaved* to sin. He has been set free to *choose to follow the Lord* and to *choose to yield to the will of the Holy Spirit.*

My little children, these things I write to you, so that you may not sin. And if anyone sins, we have an Advocate with the Father, Jesus Christ the righteous.

—1 John 2:1

What does it mean that Jesus is our Advocate? What does an advocate do?

If Jesus is our Advocate, what does this demonstrate about His love for you? What effect does it have on your attitude toward sin?

No Longer Enslaved to the Law

Paul also wrote of a second form of enslavement—the enslavement that was associated with living under the Law of Moses. He said to the Romans:

> Sin shall not have dominion over you, for you are not under law but under grace. What then? Shall we sin because we are not under law but under grace? Certainly not! Do you not know that to whom you present yourselves slaves to obey, you

are that one's slaves whom you obey, whether of sin leading to death, or of obedience leading to righteousness? But God be thanked that though you were slaves of sin, yet you obeyed from the heart that form of doctrine to which you were delivered. And having been set free from sin, you became slaves of righteousness. I speak in human terms because of the weakness of your flesh. For just as you presented your members as slaves of uncleanness, and of lawlessness leading to more lawlessness, so now present your members as slaves of righteousness for holiness.

—Romans 6:14–19

In this passage Paul admonished the Romans to recognize that the Law was for them a form of slavery. They had no choice but to serve the Law, as if serving a slave master, if they were to live in a right relationship with God. But now, Paul wrote, the grace of God has been manifested in the death and resurrection of Jesus Christ, and a person can live in the freedom of grace. And yet, Paul was quick to add, such a wonderful forgiveness compels a person to *choose* to become a slave to righteousness. The person who once governed his behavior to avoid punishment under the Law can now *choose* to do and say the right things because he loves God and desires to serve the Lord and live a holy life.

⊷ According to the Romans passage above, how is your free will involved in sin? In holiness?

47

≈ In what ways have you been set free by Jesus' gift of salvation? What are you free from? What are you free to do?

Our motivation changes when we come to Christ. Consider for a moment the person who does what is right because he is afraid of doing the wrong thing and getting caught. His behavior is good, but the motivation of his heart is suspect. In contrast, consider the person who does what is right because he deeply loves God, wants to please God, and desires to experience the fullness of God's blessings and favor. His behavior is good, but of even greater value, his motivation is godly. A person who desires to please the Lord and fulfill His commandments genuinely *loves* God and desires to live in the center of God's will.

> For you were once darkness, but now you are light in the Lord. Walk as children of light (for the fruit of the Spirit is in all goodness, righteousness, and truth), finding out what is acceptable to the Lord. And have no fellowship with the unfruitful works of darkness, but rather expose them.
>
> —Ephesians 5:8–11

☙ How does a person "find out what is acceptable to the Lord"? What is involved in that process?

☙ Why are we commanded to expose the works of darkness? How does a person do that?

Love and Redemption

The Lord desires the best for His beloved children—and the best is to be free from the captor of their souls, free from the bondage of sin's impulses, and free from a motivation rooted in guilt or shame.

A major aspect of our need for love is a need to feel *competent*—capable of accomplishing what we desire to accomplish, capable of accomplishing something that is good and lasting. God meets this need in our lives by *redeeming us*. He sets us free from the devil's hold on us so that we can act out of a pure heart and *do* the works of righteousness. He sets us free so that we *can* accomplish great things for His glory by the power of the Holy Spirit. He sets us free to function in the fullness of our God-given talents and abilities, without having those talents and abilities soiled or spoiled by sin.

God removes all the hindrances of sin that have held us back, so that we can move into the fullness of His purposes for our lives. God does not redeem us so that He can control every move we make, but so that He can *help* us become all that He gave us the potential to be and to do.

> We know that whoever is born of God does not sin; but he who has been born of God keeps himself, and the wicked one does not touch him.
>
> —1 John 5:18

☙ How are we to reconcile John's statement that "whoever is born of God does not sin" with his acknowledgement that Christians do sometimes sin?

🙠 What does this teach about the grace of God? About our response to His love?

───── 🙠 **Today and Tomorrow** 🙡 ─────

TODAY: GOD HAS REDEEMED ME FROM THE ENSLAVEMENT OF SIN SO THAT I CAN CHOOSE TO OBEY HIM.

TOMORROW: I WILL PRAYERFULLY STRIVE THIS WEEK TO EXERCISE MY FREEDOM TO OBEY GOD.

───── 🙢 ─────

God's Desire to Make You Like His Son

─────── ❧ **In This Lesson** ❧ ───────

LEARNING: WHAT DOES IT MEAN TO BE CONFORMED TO THE IMAGE OF CHRIST?

GROWING: HOW DOES A PERSON ACCOMPLISH SUCH A CONFORMATION?

A person who loves you wants you to have a great life and a great future. The person who loves you *wants* you to succeed, to maximize your potential, to achieve all that you are capable of accomplishing, to have all of your spiritual, material, and physical needs met, and to experience great love, joy, peace, and fulfillment *every* day—today, tomorrow, and forever.

That's the way that God loves you. He wants you to succeed and to be all that He has created you to be. He wants you to know the greatest fulfillment that you can possibly experience in life. He wants your needs to be met and your life to be filled with love, joy, and peace. He wants you to experience more and more of His blessings. And that is why He is determined to see you grow up spiritually into the likeness of His Son, Jesus Christ.

Jesus lived the most superlative life of any person who has ever lived. He fully succeeded in His mission on earth. He experienced the ultimate fulfillment a person can experience. He had all of His needs met—

physically, emotionally, and materially. He knew the greatest love, joy, and peace a person can ever know. Jesus said of Himself, "I have come that you might have life, and have it more abundantly" (John 10:10). Your loving heavenly Father wants you to become just like Jesus and to experience life in all of its fullness and abundance. The apostle Paul wrote to the Romans: "Whom He foreknew, He also predestined to be conformed to the image of His Son" (Rom. 8:29).

What Does It Mean to Be Conformed?

Certainly our conformity to Christ Jesus does not refer to His physical likeness. Neither can we ever be conformed to many aspects of His natural life on this earth, including His supernatural virgin birth. Neither does our conformity refer in any way to our becoming the savior of ourselves or any other person. What Christ accomplished on the cross, no other person could ever accomplish, and no person will ever be asked to die for the sins of another. Christ's death and resurrection were definitive, divine acts that only Christ could accomplish. The writers of the New Testament also make it clear that we are not called to conform ourselves to the strict practices of Judaism (Acts 15:1–30).

To what, then, are we to be conformed? We are to be conformed to the *character* of Jesus. We are to manifest His obedience to the Father, His love of God and of other people, and His character traits of joy, peace, kindness, goodness, and self-control. We are to forgive as He forgave and to call others to repentance and a newness of life just as He called those whom He encountered in His earthly ministry. We are to think as He thought, speak as He spoke, and act as He acted, motivated as He was motivated by a love for the Father.

But God forbid that I should boast except in the cross of our Lord Jesus Christ, by whom the world has been crucified to me, and I to the world. For in Christ Jesus neither circumcision nor uncircumcision avails anything, but a new creation.

—Galatians 6:14–15

❧ What are you most proud of in your life, whether openly or secretly?

❧ What does it mean to boast in the cross of Christ? What exactly was Paul boasting of when he boasted in the cross?

Adopted Sons

The apostle Paul said that we are to be conformed to the image of Christ Jesus: we are "to be conformed to the image of His Son, that He might be the firstborn among many brethren" (Rom. 8:29). Jesus is our Savior, and He is also our older brother, the firstborn in the family to which we belong. Have you ever stopped to think about what a marvelous thing it is to be part of the *family* of almighty God? God loves you and me so much that He has *adopted* us into His family.

Adoption was a very serious matter in the Roman Empire at the time of Christ. A man could disown his natural-born son, but an adopted son had full legal rights that could not be revoked. Adoption allowed a child to be a full heir of all the father had, including the use of the father's name.

> But when the fullness of the time had come, God sent forth His Son, born of a woman, born under the law, to redeem those who were under the law, that we might receive the adoption as sons. And because you are sons, God has sent forth the Spirit of His Son into your hearts, crying out, "Abba, Father!" Therefore you are no longer a slave but a son, and if a son, then an heir of God through Christ.
>
> —Galatians 4:4–7

The word *Abba* is similar to our word *daddy*. What does it reveal about God's love that we are invited to call Him "Daddy"?

⟋ What is Jesus' inheritance as God's only Son? What is your inheritance through Christ?

God's Conformation Process

The conformation process that God uses in our lives is the opposite of the world's approach.

⟋ The World's Approach to Conformation ⟍

The world's approach to conformation is a process of imitation and self-improvement.

1. Imitation of others. From the world's perspective, we conform ourselves to someone else's image by imitating that person, doing what they do, talking as they talk, adopting their mannerisms, surrounding ourselves with the possessions that the other person has, going places that the other person goes, and making choices that the other person makes. This approach is rooted in the belief that a person can *act* successful until he *is* successful. Conformation becomes a process of being a copy-cat.

Ultimately, this approach fails because, in copying a person that we perceive as successful, we tend to copy their faults and sins as much as we copy their strengths and good deeds.

 When have you tried to conform yourself to the image of another person through imitation? What were the results?

2. Improvement of self. The world's approach to conformity is a self-improvement process. The human approach says, "I can make myself into a better person, and if I work hard enough and long enough at self-improvement, I can make myself into a virtually perfect person. I can conform myself to the image of a successful person by using my willpower and changing those things that I want to change."

This approach also fails because no person can change his basic nature on his own. It takes the power of the Holy Spirit to *transform* a person from the sin nature to righteousness.

༚ Have you ever embarked on a self-improvement course? What was the long-term result?

༚ God's Approach to Conformation ༚

God's approach to conformation is a very different process—a process of indwelling and unveiling.

1. Indwelling. God's approach declares that man cannot save himself, redeem himself, or conform himself to Christ. Man's will is limited, and even the strongest willpower is too weak to accomplish anything that is life-changing and eternal. The only way for a person to achieve success is to be indwelled by the Holy Spirit. The Holy Spirit enables man to live in righteousness. The Holy Spirit's power, coupled with man's will, is true and effective *willpower.*

> And I will pray the Father, and He will give you another Helper, that He may abide with you forever—the Spirit of truth, whom the world cannot receive, because it neither sees Him nor knows Him; but you know Him, for He dwells with you and will be in you.
>
> —John 14:16–17

❧ Why is the Holy Spirit called "the Spirit of truth"? What part does truth play in conforming us to the image of Christ?

❧ Why does a person need the Holy Spirit in order to be transformed to godliness? Why can't a person transform himself?

2. *Unveiling.* God's approach to conformation is something of a subtraction process followed by an addition process. You cannot put on Christ's character without first taking off the old nature of the world.

One of the foremost roles of the Holy Spirit in our lives is to reveal those things that are displeasing to God and not in harmony with Christ's life. The Holy Spirit, in other words, reveals our base humanity to us. He shows us our fleshly nature, our pride, our sinful habits, and the errant ways in which we are dealing with other people. And He calls us to

59

repent or to change. He calls us to turn away from our old way of living and to put off the old man. Conformity ultimately involves a stripping away of all things that are not like Christ.

> Put off . . . the old man which grows corrupt according to the deceitful lusts, and be renewed in the spirit of your mind, and that you put on the new man which was created according to God, in true righteousness and holiness.
>
> —Ephesians 4:22–24

❧ Who or what is the "old man"? What does it mean to put him off? How is this accomplished, in practical terms?

❧ In what ways is Jesus the "new man"? Why is it necessary to get rid of the old man in order to become more like Christ?

✍ What does it mean to be "renewed in the spirit of your mind"? How is this done, in practical terms?

God's Commitment to Your Conformation

God is committed to your success. He has begun the work of conformation in you as a believer, and He will not abandon that work until you are mature in your faith. The work is *His* work, not ours. The glory that results is *His* glory, not ours.

> But we have this treasure in earthen vessels, that the excellence of the power may be of God and not of us.
>
> —2 Corinthians 4:7

✍ What treasure do we hold in our "earthen vessels"? What is the source of the treasure?

~ What part does the Holy Spirit play in conforming us to the image of Christ? What part do we play?

Your Awesome Destiny

As a believer in Christ Jesus, you have a great destiny. You have been given eternal life, and you are now in the process of being conformed into the very likeness of Christ Jesus. God is causing you to develop the mind of Christ and the character of Jesus, through the ongoing work of the Holy Spirit in your life. This in turn compels you to speak and to act as Jesus would if He were living in your family, your job, your church, and your community today.

> Yet indeed I also count all things loss for the excellence of the knowledge of Christ Jesus my Lord, for whom I have suffered the loss of all things, and count them as rubbish, that I may gain Christ and be found in Him, not having my own righteousness, which is from the law, but that which is through faith in Christ, the righteousness which is from God by faith.
>
> —Philippians 3:8–9

What might Paul be referring to as "my own righteousness"? Give examples of human attempts at righteousness.

What is the righteousness "which is from God by faith"? How is such righteousness attained?

Today and Tomorrow

TODAY: GOD IS ACTIVELY WORKING TO MAKE ME JUST LIKE JESUS!

TOMORROW: I WILL COOPERATE THIS WEEK WITH THE HOLY SPIRIT'S EFFORTS IN MY CONFORMATION PROCESS.

LESSON 6

God's Desire to Communicate with You

In This Lesson

LEARNING: HOW DOES GOD COMMUNICATE WITH PEOPLE IN MODERN TIMES?

GROWING: WHY WON'T GOD ANSWER MY PRAYERS?

You naturally desire to spend time and share life's experiences with someone that you love. You enjoy communicating together, both talking and listening. You look forward to seeing that person, and you hate saying good-bye. You make yourself accessible, available, and vulnerable to the one that you love.

One aspect of our great need for love is a need to feel that we are worthy, to feel that we are worth knowing, worth having around, worth conversing with, worth calling a friend. We each long to feel valuable. Ultimately, our sense of value and worthiness must be rooted in the fact that almighty God, the King of the universe, considers us *worthy* and *valuable* beyond measure.

In His great love for you, God desires to have an intimate friendship with you. He counts you worthy of His time, attention, and presence. From the very beginning God made it clear that He desired to be more than the Creator of mankind: He wanted to be a friend to mankind. His very purpose in creating man and woman was so that He might communicate with them, delight in their exploration of His creation, involve them in His creative process and plan, and enjoy their presence.

God made Himself available to Adam, and He also desired his input into His creation. We read in Genesis 2:19, "Out of the ground the LORD God formed every beast of the field and every bird of the air, and brought them to Adam to see what he would call them. And whatever Adam called each living creature, that was its name." God valued Adam's opinion!

Adam and Eve "heard the sound of the LORD God walking in the garden in the cool of the day," and they were not surprised that God was in the garden. That was a routine occurrence, a natural part of their lives. It was because they had disobeyed God's command regarding the fruit of the Tree of Knowledge of Good and Evil that they hid themselves from His presence. The Lord certainly knew where they were; nevertheless, He "called to Adam and said to him, 'Where are you?'" In doing this, He was inviting Adam to come into His presence without fear (Gen. 3:8–9). What a different outcome this story might have had if only Adam and Eve had owned up to their willful rebellion against God and asked His forgiveness, rather than attempting to justify their behavior and blame others for their sin.

The purpose for communication is to establish *relationship*. And from the beginning God has desired to have a walking-and-talking, ongoing, moment-by-moment relationship with His children. He created us for honest, heartfelt fellowship with Himself. He longs to be Father to us and to enjoy our presence as His children.

❧ Why did God take daily walks in the garden of Eden? What was His purpose?

❧ Why did Adam and Eve hide themselves from Him? What effect did sin have on their relationship to God? To one another?

There are three aspects of God's desire to communicate with us that we will cover in this lesson:

1. God's availability to us

2. God's listening ear

3. God's desire for us to be His people

God's Availability

God makes Himself infinitely accessible to His beloved children. He is never too busy or preoccupied with other people or problems to hear us and make Himself available to us. It is beyond our human ability to comprehend *how* this can be true, but we have full assurance from God's Word that it is so. Part of God's omnipotence (infinite power) is His ability to be concerned about and to rule over the smallest details. Part of God's omnipresent nature (eternal presence) is His ability to be present in each *moment* of our lives.

No believer is excluded or denied access to God at any time or for any reason. He receives all of His children at all times. Furthermore, no believer is excluded from any of the promises of God or from having access to any aspect of the Holy Spirit's power.

In His accessibility to us, the Lord is:

” patient, merciful, gracious, and full of compassion (Ps. 145:8–9).

” quick to grant salvation to any person who calls upon His name (Rom. 10:12–13; John 3:16; Joel 2:32).

” eager to have us come into His presence so that He might be our source of peace and rest (Matt. 11:28).

The Lord even gives us the language of a pure, innocent heart with which to communicate with Him (Zeph. 3:9).

For there is no distinction between Jew and Greek, for the same Lord over all is rich to all who call upon Him. For *"whoever calls on the name of the LORD shall be saved."*

—Romans 10:12–13

❧ Paul uses the term "Greek" to refer to all people who are not Jews. Why was there originally a distinction between Jews and everyone else? Why did Jesus remove that distinction?

❧ Who can attain eternal life, according to these verses? Why do some people not take advantage of God's generous availability?

God's Listening Ear

King David had absolutely no doubt that the Lord heard him when he prayed. He prayed with full expectation that God would hear and answer:

> LORD, I cry out to You;
> Make haste to me!
> Give ear to my voice when I cry out to You.
> Let my prayer be set before You as incense,
> The lifting up of my hands as the evening sacrifice.

> —Psalm 141:1–2

In another psalm we read, "I said to the LORD: 'You are my God; hear the voice of my supplications, O Lord. O GOD the Lord, the strength of my salvation'" (Ps. 140:6–7). David believed that God would hear and answer his prayer in a way that was beneficial to David and to the furtherance of God's purposes.

☙ When you pray, are you consciously expecting God to listen? To answer?

69

☙ Have you ever felt that God was not available or not listening? What caused you to feel that way? What does Scripture say about it?

☙ Every Prayer is Answered ❧

God hears and answers every prayer. "But," you may say, "I have prayed lots of prayers that God didn't answer." Be honest with yourself. Are you saying that God didn't answer or that He didn't answer in the way that *you* desired? The truth is that God answers all prayers, but according to His goodness and His eternal purposes.

The petitions we make out of our finite understanding are answered out of the abundance of God's infinite wisdom and eternal perspective. God's answers to us are "yes," "no," "not now," and "if ... then." When we pray according to His will for us—which is always for our eternal good—His answer is always "yes," although we may not receive His answer in the timing or the way that we had imagined. Anytime we petition Him for something that is contrary to our eternal good, His answer is going to be "no." At times the Lord gives us a yes answer but asks us to wait for His answer to be manifested. At other times He gives us a yes answer *if* we will meet certain conditions that He has established in His Word. When you pray, look for God's answer to *you*. Listen for it. He hears your prayers and responds to them. But very often we do not wait in His presence for His response.

❧ When has the Lord said yes to your prayers? When has He said no?

❧ When have you seen a prayer answered after a period of waiting? Why did the Lord want you to wait?

King Solomon had a clear understanding that God heard and responded to all prayer. I encourage you to read the prayer that he prayed at the time the temple in Jerusalem was completed (1 Kings 8:22–54). After Solomon had finished his prayer, he stood and blessed the people of Israel and said:

> Blessed be the LORD, who has given rest to His people Israel, according to all that He promised. There has not failed one word of all His good promise ... May the LORD our God be with us, as He was with our fathers. May He not leave us nor forsake us, that He may incline our hearts to Himself, to walk in all His ways, and to keep His commandments and His statutes and His judgments, which He commanded our fathers. And may these words of mine, with which I have made supplication before the LORD, be near the LORD our God day and night, that He may maintain the cause of His servant and the cause of His people Israel, as each day may require, that all the peoples of the earth may know that the LORD is God; there is no other.
>
> —1 Kings 8:56–60

≈. According to Solomon's prayer, what are some of the reasons for God's presence in our lives?

✎ What part does our obedience play in God's answers to our prayers?

✎ God Also Listens to the Heart ✎

God listens to our verbal prayers—our spoken expressions of petition, praise, and thanksgiving—but He also listens to our hearts. He knows our thoughts. He is aware of how we feel. He knows our unspoken needs, dreams, wishes, hopes, and desires. God listens to *what you say* and also to *who you are*. He knows you completely because He pays attention to every detail of your life, inside and out. And He listens to *you*—all of you—with compassion.

> For the word of God is living and powerful, and sharper than any two-edged sword, piercing even to the division of soul and spirit, and of joints and marrow, and is a discerner of the thoughts and intents of the heart. And there is no creature hidden from His sight, but all things are naked and open to the eyes of Him to whom we must give account.
>
> —Hebrews 4:12–13

 In what way is Scripture "living and powerful"? How is it "sharper than any two-edged sword"?

 How do you feel knowing that nothing is hidden from God, not even your deepest secrets? In what ways is that a sobering realization? In what ways is it freeing?

God's Desire for Us to Be His People

God has a great desire to be with us and to bless us. His Word to His people throughout the ages has been, "I will walk among you and be your God, and you shall be My people" (Leviticus 26:12).

For many centuries the Israelites had an understanding that God was their husband; He was the One who cared for them, protected them, nurtured them, provided for them, and called them by name. In the New Testament those who followed Christ Jesus understood themselves to be the bride of Christ. God's people have always recognized that God desires to be in the closest, most intimate relationship with them.

> You are My friends if you do whatever I command you. No longer do I call you servants, for a servant does not know what his master is doing; but I have called you friends, for all things that I heard from My Father I have made known to you.
>
> —John 15:14–15

What is the difference between a servant (such as a restaurant waiter) and a friend? Which role do you tend to embrace in your relationship with God?

75

∽ What is required of us if we are to be called Jesus' friends?

∽ Today and Tomorrow ∾

TODAY: THE LORD ANSWERS EVERY PRAYER, AND EVERY ANSWER IS THE BEST ANSWER.

TOMORROW: I WILL ASK THE LORD TO HELP ME UNDERSTAND HIS ANSWERS TO MY PRAYERS THIS WEEK.

Our Response to God's Love:

A Passion to Know God

❧ In This Lesson ☙

LEARNING: WHAT CAN I DO TO EXPERIENCE GOD'S LOVE MORE FULLY?

GROWING: HOW CAN A PERSON KNOW GOD HERE AND NOW?

God knows everything about you. He knows your strengths, abilities, and accomplishments. He knows your desires, dreams, hopes, and goals. He knows what thrills your soul and what breaks your heart. He knows your past, present, and future. And He loves you as fully as He knows you!

But what do you know about God? Do you know Him well? Do you know His strengths, abilities, and accomplishments? Do you know what God desires? Do you know what pleases God and what breaks His heart?

As believers, we are to have a *passion* for God. In the world today, passion is often related to sexual desire, but the true meaning of the word is "an overwhelming, strong desire," which can be a strong desire for matters of the spirit. Believers are to have an urgency, a fervor, a zealous desire for the Lord and everything related to Him.

The apostle Paul expressed his passion for the Lord as a pressing toward the "upward call of God in Christ Jesus" (Phil. 3:14). Paul was determined to know Christ, completely forgetting his old life and reaching toward all the things that the Lord had for him in the present and the future. He said of himself, "I was zealous for God" (Acts 22:3).

Phinehas, the son of Eleazar and the grandson of Aaron, the priest of the Israelites, was noted by God for his zeal. Read God's promise regarding him:

> Behold, I give to him My covenant of peace; and it shall be to him and his descendants after him a covenant of an everlasting priesthood, because he was zealous for his God, and made atonement for the children of Israel.

> —Numbers 25:12–13

What does it mean to be zealous for God? Give practical examples.

✍ What things please God? What things break His heart?

✍ Spend some time right now praising God for His many strengths and accomplishments.

Our Knowledge of the Lord

Our passion to know God is rooted in a desire to understand who He is, how He works, and what He desires. This is not head knowledge alone, but knowledge that bears itself out in our experiences with the Lord. It is not a knowing *about* the Lord, but genuinely *knowing* the Lord—anticipating what the Lord would say or do in any given situation, feeling the presence and power of the Lord operating in us, and responding to life in our attitude as the Lord Himself responds.

The apostle Paul called the Colossians to pursue such a knowledge of the Lord. He prayed that their "hearts may be encouraged, being knit together in love, and attaining to all riches of the full assurance of understanding, to the knowledge of the mystery of God, both of the Father and of Christ, in whom are hidden all the treasures of wisdom and knowledge" (Col. 2:2–3). He longed for the Colossians to be "rooted and built up in Him and established in the faith ... abounding in it" (Col. 2:7).

Those who have a passion for the Lord place top priority on knowing Him. They value their relationship with the Lord above all other relationships, even more than their passion for a spouse or children, a job, or a ministry. They have a passion to know Christ Jesus as intimately and as fully as possible. Paul wrote:

> I also count all things loss for the excellence of the knowledge of Christ Jesus my Lord, for whom I have suffered the loss of all things, and count them as rubbish, that I may gain Christ.
>
> —Philippians 3:8

What things have you lost or sacrificed in pursuit of a deeper relationship with Christ?

What things might be holding you back at present from knowing God more deeply?

Knowing the Greatness of the Lord

Those who have a passion to know God have a growing understanding of the greatness of God. They are able to grasp the vast, incomprehensible, mysterious infinity of God's wisdom, power, presence, and love. And the more they know the greatness of God, the more they value the love that God extends toward them. They have a growing joy in their hearts and a greater capacity to proclaim, "What a God is He who loves me!" King David blessed the Lord before the Israelites, saying:

Blessed are You, LORD God of Israel....
Yours, O Lord, is the greatness,
The power and the glory,
The victory and the majesty;
For all that is in heaven and in earth is Yours;
Yours is the kingdom, O Lord,
And You are exalted as head over all.

Both riches and honor come from You,
And You reign over all.
In Your hand is power and might;
In Your hand it is to make great
And to give strength to all.
Now therefore, our God,
We thank You
And praise Your glorious name.

—1 Chronicles 29:10–13

∝ Put David's prayer into your own words below, then spend time in prayer.

Not that I have already attained, or am already perfected; but I press on, that I may lay hold of that for which Christ Jesus has also laid hold of me. Brethren, I do not count myself to have apprehended; but one thing I do, forgetting those things which are behind and reaching forward to those things which are ahead, I press toward the goal for the prize of the upward call of God in Christ Jesus.

—Philippians 3:12–14

∽ What things are you "reaching forward" towards in your vision of the future? What things might the Lord want you to be reaching toward?

∽ What past events in your life might it be helpful to forget? How can memories of the past hinder your walk in the future?

☙ What does it mean to "press toward the goal for the prize of the upward call of God in Christ Jesus"? What goal did Paul strive for? What prize?

Knowing the Goodness of the Lord

Those who have a passion to know God discover and rediscover the goodness of the Lord in countless ways, in countless situations, and at countless times. The more they discover the goodness of the Lord, the more they see that God's goodness and God's love are inseparable. He loves us in *good* ways, and His goodness is always expressed with love toward those who seek Him with all their hearts.

☙ When have you experienced the goodness of God in your own life?

84

~ When have you discovered in hindsight that the Lord had been good, even though you hadn't seen it at the time?

Knowing the Lord Through Identification with Him

The main ways that we know the Lord are through prayer, praise, an understanding of His Word, and our identification with the Lord's life: His struggles and sufferings, as well as His victories.

~ A Knowledge of His Suffering ~

The longer we walk with Christ and the more intimately we come to know Him, the more we are likely to experience rejection and alienation by the world. We are going to be misunderstood and ridiculed just as He was. We are going to be criticized as He was. We are going to be tempted as He was, tempted to pursue those things that satisfy self, including power, fame, and the adoration of others. We are going to be persecuted for our faith, sometimes in very painful ways. And some of us are going to be martyred for our faith, just as Christians have been martyred through the ages.

Perhaps no other person ever identified so completely with Christ as the apostle Paul. His life was not immune from trouble. Far from it! He was persecuted often for Christ's sake. He wrote to the Corinthians:

> From the Jews five times I received forty stripes minus one. Three times I was beaten with rods; once I was stoned; three times I was shipwrecked; a night and a day I have been in the deep; in journeys often, in perils of waters, in perils of robbers, in perils of my own countrymen, in perils of the Gentiles, in perils in the city, in perils in the wilderness, in perils in the sea, in perils among false brethren; in weariness and toil, in sleeplessness often, in hunger and thirst, in fastings often, in cold and nakedness—besides the other things, what comes upon me daily: my deep concern for all the churches.... And lest I should be exalted above measure by the abundance of the revelations, a thorn in the flesh was given to me, a messenger of Satan to buffet me, lest I be exalted above measure. Concerning this thing I pleaded with the Lord three times that it might depart from me. And He said to me, "My grace is sufficient for you, for My strength is made perfect in weakness." Therefore most gladly I will rather boast in my infirmities, that the power of Christ may rest upon me. Therefore I take pleasure in infirmities, in reproaches, in needs, in persecutions, in distresses, for Christ's sake. For when I am weak, then I am strong.
>
> —2 Corinthians 11:24–28; 12:7–10

When have you been persecuted for the sake of Christ? How did you respond?

👡 What does it mean to boast in one's infirmities? When have you experienced God's power in spite of your own weaknesses?

Christ does not immunize us from troubles and struggles, rather the Holy Spirit empowers us to confront, overcome, and endure troubles and struggles victoriously. Great rewards go to those who overcome! (See Revelation 2–3 and note the repeated phrase "he who overcomes.")

👡 A Knowledge of His Victories 👡

The more we seek to know the Lord and have a passion for living out His life on earth, the more we are also going to know victories and triumphs in the spiritual realm. Jesus told His disciples about the life that they would experience after His resurrection and after He sent the Holy Spirit to them:

> Most assuredly, I say to you, whatever you ask the Father in My name He will give you. Until now you have asked nothing in My name. Ask, and you will receive, that your joy may be full.

> —John 16:23–24

Jesus promised His disciples that they would:

    ❧ experience great personal protection against evil and power over evil (Mark 16:15–18).

    ❧ have power to loose people to receive God's blessings (Matt. 18:18).

    ❧ receive great answer to their prayers (Matt. 18:19–20).

    ❧ have effective and fruitful ministries marked by works that would exceed His (John 14:12–14; John 15:16).

To know the Lord is to identify so fully with His life that you experience what the Lord experienced on this earth: sufferings and great victories. It is through our total identification with His life that we learn the lessons that mold our nature and character for all eternity. It is through our total identification with Him that we learn even more about God's great love for us, that God loves us *always*, regardless of the circumstances around us. We learn the sustaining and encouraging power of God's love!

Remember the word that I said to you, "A servant is not greater than his master." If they persecuted Me, they will also persecute you. If they kept My word, they will keep yours also. But all these things they will do to you for My name's sake, because they do not know Him who sent Me.

—John 15:20–21

🕮 What does it mean that a servant is not greater than his master? What sorts of things would a household servant share in common with his employer?

🕮 What things does a Christian share in common with Jesus—both good and bad? How can such sharing—good and bad—deepen your understanding of His character?

❧ Today and Tomorrow ❧

TODAY: LOVE IS A TWO-WAY RELATIONSHIP, AND I NEED TO KNOW GOD INTIMATELY TO UNDERSTAND HIS LOVE.

TOMORROW: I WILL ASK THE LORD THIS WEEK TO HELP ME UNDERSTAND HIM BETTER.

❧ Notes and Prayer Requests: ❧

Our Response to God's Love:

A Passion to Obey God

☙ In This Lesson ❧

Learning: What is a proper response to the love of God?

Growing: Where can I gain a greater passion for Him?

∞

Those who know the greatness and goodness of God, who seek to identify fully with Christ's life, have a great passion to obey God. To know God is to *serve* God. Obedience is active, not passive. It is a living out of what we know to be true, right, and good. It is to follow the Lord daily, saying and doing what Jesus would do if He were living our lives today. It is displaying the truth of God in the deeds of our everyday lives. Obedience is a total submission to what *God* desires, not what we desire out of our sensual lusts, greed, and pride.

Our heavenly Father places high value on obedience. He prefers it even to sacrifice or to the outward expressions of worship (1 Sam. 15:22). In fact, the obedient way in which we live our lives is the ultimate expression of worship and service (Prov. 21:3). He wants us to be hearers of His Word and also *doers* of it (James 1:22).

So Samuel said: "Has the LORD as great delight in burnt offer-
ings and sacrifices, as in obeying the voice of the LORD? Behold, to obey is better than sacrifice, and to heed than the fat
of rams."

—1 Samuel 15:22

❧ When have you obeyed God's word at significant cost to yourself? In what ways was this act of obedience more meaningful
than other forms of worship?

❧ Why does God place such high value on obedience, even more
than Sunday morning worship attendance?

A passion to obey God is generally expressed in a Christian's life in these three ways:

1. a passion to know the Bible

2. a passion to live in righteousness

3. a passion to receive daily direction from the Lord

Ultimately, these three desires—for God's Word, righteousness, and daily guidance work together—work together. The more we know God's Word, the greater our understanding will be of righteousness and how the Holy Spirit works in our lives. The more we trust the Holy Spirit, the more He reminds us of God's Word and leads us into paths of righteousness. The more we desire to live in right standing before the Father, the more we will want to read His Word and listen for His voice.

A Knowledge of the Bible

To know what God requires of us, we must know what God has commanded His people to do. God's commandments have not changed through the ages; they have not been altered according to culture, custom, or technological advances. God's Word is absolute, and it is enduring. You can have a great desire to obey the Lord, but unless you know what the Lord has commanded His people to do, you will fail in your obedience.

How sweet are Your words to my taste, sweeter than honey to my mouth! Through Your precepts I get understanding; therefore I hate every false way. Your word is a lamp to my feet and a light to my path.

—Psalm 119:103–105

～ When have you found God's word to be "sweeter than honey"?

～ In what ways is God's word like a lamp to your feet? How does it act as a light on your path? What is needed for such lamps to be effective to the person walking?

A Desire for Righteousness

Throughout the Bible we find the word *righteousness*. Very simply, living in righteousness is doing what is right before the Lord. It is keeping His commandments and statutes. It is turning away from sin and toward what is holy and acceptable to the Lord. The writer to the Hebrews encouraged believers to:

Lay aside every weight, and the sin which so easily ensnares us, and let us run with endurance the race that is set before us, looking unto Jesus, the author and finisher of our faith.

—Hebrews 12:1–2

❧ In what sense is Jesus both the author and finisher of your faith? What is your part in the process?

❧ What sorts of "weight" might need to be laid aside in your life? What areas of sin do you find yourself easily ensnared in?

Sin produces guilt, which is a terrible burden to the soul. Sin is also a snare to us, taking us captive and holding us back from doing those things that would bring God's blessing into our lives. It is up to us—and within the ability of our wills—to *choose* not to sin. Once we have made this decision within our wills, the Holy Spirit enables us with consistency and power *not* to sin. Laying aside sin and pursuing obedience *is* righteousness.

Trust and Obey the Holy Spirit

To have a passion for obedience is to have a deep desire to receive direction from the Holy Spirit daily. To obey is to walk in His ways, step by step, trusting that God is leading you and that He will correct you should you make an error in hearing His voice clearly. Our reliance upon the Holy Spirit requires two things of us:

1. Observing what God is doing. Many Christians go through life with tunnel vision. They fail to catch the big picture of what God is doing in their personal lives, in the lives of others around them, and in the world as a whole.

2. Frequently asking God, "What's my role?" As we catch a glimpse of the good work that God has done, is doing, and desires to do in us, we need to ask frequently, "What do You desire of me, Lord? What should my next step be? Where do You want me to go? What do You want me to do and say?"

> Set a guard, O LORD, over my mouth; keep watch over the door of my lips. Do not incline my heart to any evil thing, to practice wicked works with men who work iniquity; and do not let me eat of their delicacies.
>
> —Psalm 141:3–4

❧ When have you wished in hindsight that you had kept your mouth shut? When has the Lord providentially prevented you from saying something hurtful?

❧ What sort of "delicacies" does the world use to tempt you? What worldly things might the Lord want you to refrain from?

Our passion to obey God increases the more we experience God's love at work in our lives. To know God's love is to know that God will never lead us into any activity that will bring us spiritual harm. We can trust God to take us into greater avenues of ministry and a more satisfying relationship with Him and with others who love and serve Him.

In like manner, the more we know God's love, the more we will desire to obey Him. Our love for God compels us to serve Him. Our obedience enables us to know His love to an ever-expanding depth and breadth and to experience more and more of His blessings. The result is a cycle of obedience and love that continues to grow from now until eternity.

> But be doers of the word, and not hearers only, deceiving your-selves. For if anyone is a hearer of the word and not a doer, he is like a man observing his natural face in a mirror; for he ob-serves himself, goes away, and immediately forgets what kind of man he was. But he who looks into the perfect law of liberty and continues in it, and is not a forgetful hearer but a doer of the work, this one will be blessed in what he does.
>
> —James 1:22–25

In what ways do we deceive ourselves if we study God's word but do not strive to obey it? Why does Paul use a mirror as a metaphor for this practice?

☙ Are there areas of God's word that you have not been fully obeying? What will you do this week to obey God more fully?

☙ Today and Tomorrow ☙

TODAY: THE MORE I OBEY GOD, THE MORE PASSIONATE I WILL BECOME TOWARD HIM.

TOMORROW: I WILL ASK THE LORD TO INCREASE MY LOVE AND SHOW ME AREAS OF OBEDIENCE.

LESSON 9

Our Response to God's Love:

A Passion to Serve Others

---------------- ❧ **In This Lesson** ❧ ----------------

LEARNING: WHAT EFFECT SHOULD GOD'S LOVE HAVE IN MY DAILY LIFE?

GROWING: HOW AM I TO RESPOND TO PEOPLE WHO ANNOY ME?

---------------------- ❧ ----------------------

Do you receive greater joy from being served by others or from serving others? Those who experience the love of God in their lives find great joy in loving others. They are eager to share with others what God has placed in their hearts. And love is far more than a feeling or an emotion; it is an act of *giving* or serving that is born of the will.

The apostle Paul wrote to the Philippians:

> Let this mind be in you which was also in Christ Jesus, who, being in the form of God, did not consider it robbery to be equal with God, but made Himself of no reputation, taking the form of a bondservant, and coming in the likeness of men. And being found in appearance as a man, He humbled Himself and became obedient to the point of death, even the death of the cross.
>
> —Philippians 2:5–8

In what costly ways did Jesus demonstrate active love for others?

What role does obedience play in such love?

Serving God is the normal lifestyle of the believer in Christ Jesus. The believer does not live for *himself* but seeks to pour out himself to others. The apostle Paul reminded the Corinthians that, while he was preaching the gospel to them, he did not take wages from them as he had from other churches. He wrote, "I was a burden to no one ... in everything I kept myself from being burdensome to you, and so I will keep myself." And then Paul asked rhetorically, "Why? Because I do not love you? God knows!" (2 Cor. 11:9, 11). Paul freely poured out his time, energy, and knowledge of Christ Jesus to the Corinthians because he loved them. He sought to *serve* far more than to be served. He sought to *give* far more than to receive.

✍ Recall several people who have given to you freely, without expecting any return. How was God's love manifested through them to you?

The Greatest Servant of All

Without a doubt, Jesus Christ is the greatest Servant who ever lived. No other person has ever given so much to so many, so generously and so sacrificially. In all ways, Jesus is our role model for loving service to others. Read again the account of Jesus at the Last Supper, when He literally took on the garments of a servant and performed the tasks of a servant in ministering to His disciples:

> Now before the Feast of the Passover, when Jesus knew that His hour had come that He should depart from this world to the Father, having loved His own who were in the world, He loved them to the end.
>
> And supper being ended ... Jesus, knowing that the Father had given all things into His hands, and that He had come from God and was going to God, rose from supper and laid aside His garments, took a towel and girded Himself. After that, He poured water into a basin and began to wash the disciples' feet, and to wipe them with the towel with which He was girded....

So when He had washed their feet, taken His garments, and sat down again, He said to them, "Do you know what I have done to you? You call Me Teacher and Lord, and you say well, for so I am. If I then, your Lord and Teacher, have washed your feet, you also ought to wash one another's feet. For I have given you an example, that you should do as I have done to you. Most assuredly, I say to you, a servant is not greater than his master; nor is he who is sent greater than he who sent him. If you know these things, blessed are you if you do them."

—John 13:1–5, 12–17

Why did Jesus wash the feet of His disciples? What was He trying to accomplish?

Washing feet was the job of the lowest household servant in Jesus' day. What forms of service might be comparable today?

As believers in Christ Jesus, we are called to serve others as Christ served the disciples, even if it means giving up our pride and selfish desires or doing something for another person that we might consider menial, undignified, or beneath us. Service to others is *self-sacrificial*. Paul reminded the believers of this in writing to the Romans: "I beseech you therefore, brethren, by the mercies of God, that you present your bodies a living sacrifice, holy, acceptable to God, which is your reasonable service" (Rom. 12:1).

> Whoever desires to become great among you shall be your servant. And whoever of you desires to be first shall be slave of all. For even the Son of Man did not come to be served, but to serve, and to give His life a ransom for many.
>
> —Mark 10:43–45

What rights does a slave have? What sorts of tasks are performed by slaves and servants?

Why did Jesus command His followers to become slaves and servants? Why is this necessary to become great in His kingdom?

The Nature of the Service We Give

The service we give to others in the name of the Lord should always have these characteristics:

ꙮ *Humility.* The true servant gives to others in kindness and humility. He knows that all of his abilities are an outpouring of God's love in his life, and he delights in using his talents and gifts to help others as an expression of both his love and God's love.

ꙮ *Expressed with righteousness, peace, and joy.* Those who serve others in Christ's name do so because it is the right thing to do before the Lord. They serve with peace in their hearts and joy on their faces. They give, seeking nothing in return, but they serve as if serving the Lord Himself, with reverence and awe.

ꙮ *Expressed with a desire for good in the other person's life.* Those who serve the Lord always seek the will of God for the other person, which is whatever promotes an eternal blessing and benefit in that person's life.

ꙮ *An expression of love for our heavenly Father.* A love for the Father was what motivated Jesus to serve others. This same love for our heavenly Father should be what motivates us to serve. In serving others, we are literally pouring out our lives before God as a living sacrifice, just as Jesus Christ poured out His life as our sacrifice on the cross.

As you have read these traits of loving service, you no doubt have recognized that these are the very traits of Christ's life and the love that He expressed to others. As Christ loved and served His heavenly Father and His disciples, so we are to love and serve God and others.

Be of the same mind toward one another. Do not set your mind on high things, but associate with the humble. Do not be wise in your own opinion. Repay no one evil for evil. Have regard for good things in the sight of all men. If it is possible, as much as depends on you, live peaceably with all men.

—Romans 12:16–18

❧ What does it mean to "set your mind on high things"? Give some examples.

❧ Who are "the humble"? What might it mean in your life to associate with them?

Our Service Brings Glory to God

Our service to others is ultimately service to God, since our faithfulness, worship, and loving acts of giving bring glory to God. Our service causes others to have higher regard for God and to worship Him with renewed fervor. The person who loves God delights in bringing glory to the Lord!

King Darius reluctantly ordered Daniel to be thrown into the lions' den, after being tricked into signing a foolish law. The next morning the king visited the lions' den. There, he cried out "with a lamenting voice," saying, "Daniel, servant of the living God, has your God, whom you serve continually, been able to deliver you from the lions?" Daniel replied from the lions' den, "My God sent His angel and shut the lions' mouths, so that they have not hurt me, because I was found innocent before Him; and also, O king, I have done no wrong before you" (Dan. 6).

Here is how King Darius responded to that great miracle:

> I make a decree that in every dominion of my kingdom
> men must tremble and fear before the God of Daniel.
> For He is the living God,
> And steadfast forever;
> His kingdom is the one which shall not be destroyed,
> And His dominion shall endure to the end.
> He delivers and rescues,
> And He works signs and wonders
> In heaven and on earth,
> Who has delivered Daniel from the power of the lions.
>
> —Daniel 6:26–27

Daniel brought glory to God by his faithful *service*, faithful service in worshiping God and faithful service in the performance of his duties for the king.

> As bondservants of Christ, doing the will of God from the heart, with goodwill doing service, as to the Lord, and not to men, knowing that whatever good anyone does, he will receive the same from the Lord, whether he is a slave or free.

> —Ephesians 6:6–8

➳ What is the difference between performing a service "as to the Lord" and doing it "to men"? How is one's mindset different? How is the service different?

➳ When has someone served you with goodwill? When has someone served you grudgingly, with a bad attitude? What was it like to receive each act of service?

The Lord's Response to Our Service

The Lord always responds to our heartfelt and generous service to others with an outpouring of blessing. Jesus taught, "Give, and it will be given to you: good measure, pressed down, shaken together, and running over will be put into your bosom. For with the same measure that you use, it will be measured back to you" (Luke 6:38). Jesus also said, "If anyone serves Me, let him follow Me; and where I am, there My servant will be also. If anyone serves Me, him My Father will honor" (John 12:26).

The Lord does not love us *because* we serve Him—He loves us unconditionally—but the Lord does love the fact that we serve Him. He loves our response to His love and the fact that we are giving to others from our hearts. He honors our service with His blessings. Conversely, we do not serve others because we seek a reward from God. Rather, we serve others because we have experienced God's love and we desire to express God's love.

When we serve others, we must always do so motivated by God's love. We must serve *expecting* nothing in return. At the same time, we can be assured that God *will* reward our service by giving us an abundance of the very things that we need the most, both now and in eternity. When it becomes our very nature to love others and serve them, we truly are reflecting the nature of the Lord, which is to love and serve. It is from the Lord, and Him alone, that all rewards for service ultimately come.

And whatever you do, do it heartily, as to the Lord and not to men, knowing that from the Lord you will receive the reward of the inheritance; for you serve the Lord Christ.

—Colossians 3:23–24

∽ What does it mean to do something heartily? How is hearty service different from half-hearted service? Give some real-life examples.

∽ If Jesus were visiting your home, how would you wait on Him? What sort of host would you be? How would your service to Him differ from everyday service to others?

If someone says, "I love God," and hates his brother, he is a liar; for he who does not love his brother whom he has seen, how can he love God whom he has not seen? And this commandment we have from Him: that he who loves God must love his brother also.

—1 John 4:20–21

❧ Who is your brother? Which of your brothers do you love freely? Which do you find more difficult to love?

❧ In what ways do we demonstrate the depth of our love for God by the ways that we treat other people?

❧ Today and Tomorrow ☙

TODAY: GOD LOVED ME EVEN WHEN I DID NOT LOVE HIM, AND I MUST IMITATE THAT LOVE.

TOMORROW: I WILL ASK THE LORD TO TEACH ME THIS WEEK HOW TO LOVE OTHERS AS HE LOVES ME.

❧ Notes and Prayer Requests: ☙

Lesson 10

Our Response to God's Love:

A Passion to Proclaim Christ

ᕦ In This Lesson ᕤ

LEARNING: AM I RESPONSIBLE FOR TELLING OTHERS ABOUT CHRIST?

GROWING: WHAT IF I DON'T KNOW WHAT TO SAY?

Those who are in love can hardly keep quiet about it. They delight in talking about the one they love and in telling what their beloved says and does. Those who have experienced God's love can hardly keep quiet about God. They delight in talking about Him. They are quick to quote His Word and to tell of His marvelous works—not only in their lives, but also in the lives of others.

The disciples of Jesus could not help but proclaim who Jesus was and what Jesus had done on the cross. Peter and John were arrested and persecuted for healing a man in the name of Jesus, and they responded, "We cannot but speak the things which we have seen and heard" (Acts 4:20).

The disciples had a great desire to persuade others to believe in God, to accept Jesus as their Savior, and to open themselves to the healing power of God's love. Paul said to King Agrippa, "I would to God that not only you, but also all who hear me today, might become both almost and altogether such as I am, except for these chains" (Acts. 26:29). Paul had a burning desire to persuade others to receive and experience all they could of Jesus Christ.

> But he who prophesies speaks edification and exhortation and comfort to men.

> —1 Corinthians 14:3

~ Define each of these words:

Edification:

Exhortation:

Comfort:

~ What part does each play in telling others about Christ?

The Proclamations That We Make

We make proclamations about Jesus Christ and God's love for us both in word and in deed. Our testimony or witness for the Lord is not limited to what we say about Jesus. Our witness is our entire life—the things we do and *don't* do, the way that we regard strangers and treat family members and friends, the manner in which we make choices and decisions, the associations we make, the tasks we undertake, the ways in which we handle criticism and persecution. Anything we do that is observed by another person is part of our witness for the Lord. Our *lives* proclaim what we believe as much as our words give witness to Christ.

🌶 Who has been the most effective witness to you about God's love and plan of forgiveness? What made that person's witness so effective?

Though I speak with the tongues of men and of angels, but have not love, I have become sounding brass or a clanging cymbal. And though I have the gift of prophecy, and understand all mysteries and all knowledge, and though I have all faith, so that I could remove mountains, but have not love, I am nothing.

—1 Corinthians 13:1–2

ॐ When has someone told you the truth in love? When has someone told you the truth in anger? How did you react to the truth in each case?

ॐ How does a person show love when preaching the gospel? Give real-life examples.

ॐ What We Have Experienced ॐ

The apostle John said that Jesus only spoke what He had seen and heard from the Father. John wrote, "He who comes from heaven is above all. And what He has seen and heard, that He testifies ... He whom God has sent speaks the words of God" (John 3:31–32, 34). Jesus spoke from His *experience* with the Father, and so must we. We are to speak what we have come to know personally about God's truth and God's love.

The strongest witness that we can ever give for Jesus Christ is to say, "This is what He did for me." The strongest testimony that we can give about God's love is, "This is how He loved me." Nobody can argue effectively against what *you* have experienced of Christ. Take confidence in what *you know from experience* about the truth of God's Word, the sacrifice of Jesus Christ on the cross, and the way in which God expresses His unconditional love.

> I speak what I have seen with My Father, and you do what you have seen with your father.
>
> —John 8:38

🔊 What relationship did Jesus have with God the Father? What qualified Him to speak the Father's words?

🔊 What qualifies you to speak God's words to others? How can you become more qualified?

❧ What God Tells Us to Say ☙

The prophets in the Old Testament all knew that they were required to speak whatever the Lord commanded them to speak, even if it didn't please others. King Ahab once gathered four hundred prophets together to ask them if he should go to war against his enemy. They all said that the Lord would give Ahab victory in the battle. Then a messenger was sent to the prophet Micaiah. The messenger said, "'Now listen, the words of the prophets with one accord encourage the king. Therefore please let your word be like the word of one of them, and speak encouragement.' And Micaiah said, 'As the LORD lives, whatever my God says, that I will speak'" (2 Chron. 18:12–13).

Regardless of what others may *want* us to proclaim to them, we must always be faithful in speaking *what the Lord gives us to say to them*. It may be a word of encouragement, or it may be a word of admonishment. It may be a word of wisdom or knowledge or a prophetic word. Whatever the nature of the message, we must listen closely to the One who gives the message and convey it accurately and faithfully.

When we experience God's love, we have no fear in proclaiming the Word of the Lord. As John wrote, "There is no fear in love; but perfect love casts out fear, because fear involves torment" (1 John 4:18).

> You will be brought before governors and kings for My sake, as a testimony to them and to the Gentiles. But when they deliver you up, do not worry about how or what you should speak. For it will be given to you in that hour what you should speak; for it is not you who speak, but the Spirit of your Father who speaks in you.
>
> —Matthew 10:18–20

How do these verses offer encouragement about sharing God's word with others? What sobering responsibility do they also suggest?

What role does the Holy Spirit play in sharing the gospel with others? What role do you play?

Look for Opportunities to Proclaim Christ to Others

Our witness for Christ Jesus is not passive. We must actively seek opportunities to proclaim God's love and His plan for forgiveness. We must actively listen to the Holy Spirit and follow His directions so that we are in the right place at the right time to give a witness to Christ.

One of the great examples of this is the story of Philip, who was told by an angel of the Lord to go south along the road from Jerusalem to Gaza. As he went, Philip encountered a man from Ethiopia who was on his way home after worshiping in Jerusalem. He was sitting in his chariot reading Isaiah, and the Holy Spirit spoke in Philip's heart, "Go near and overtake this chariot." Philip ran to him and said, "Do you understand what you are reading?" The man replied, "How can I, unless someone guides me?" He asked Philip to sit with him in his chariot, and as they sat there together, "Philip opened his mouth, and beginning at this Scripture [from Isa. 53], preached Jesus to him" (Acts 8:26–35). The Ethiopian man believed in Christ Jesus and was baptized that very day!

What role did the Holy Spirit play in the Ethiopian's conversion? What role did Philip play?

Are you willing to be available to God at a moment's notice, as Philip was? To move out of your comfort zone as Philip did?

Are you listening closely today to how the Holy Spirit may direct you to speak to someone about the love of God and His plan for eternal salvation through Jesus Christ? Are you actively seeking opportunities to proclaim Christ Jesus to the world through your words and deeds? The fact is, when we truly *know* the love of God *poured into* our hearts (Rom. 5:5), we will desire to *pour out* that love at every opportunity by what we say and what we do. We will long for others to know God's love as we have known it. We will be quick to proclaim His goodness, His love, His mercy, and His forgiveness to all we encounter.

How Much Love?

None of us can ever fully grasp the love of God. It is infinite, and we can never know the full extent of God's love to us. Nevertheless, we can be assured that His love is unending, rich, and wonderful. It is out of the unfathomable depths of His love that He gives to His children those things that are "exceedingly abundantly above all that we ask or think" (Eph. 3:20).

Many Christians believe in God's love—that God is love, He loves people, and He loves with an infinite capacity to love. They have difficulty believing, however, that God loves *them,* individually and personally. Let me assure you once again that God loves *you*. With the full capacity of His love, He loves *you*. With all of His heart, He loves *you*. With a great desire to be with you, work in you, and work through you, He loves *you*. With great tenderness and mercy, great compassion and kindness, He loves *you*. With a desire for your eternal best, He loves *you*. And He will always love *you*.

Once you begin to understand with your mind and receive with your heart that God loves *you*, you will begin to experience the transforming power of God in your life. His love heals us, renews us, and makes us whole. His love becomes the ultimate haven of rest for our souls, both now and forever.

> Go therefore and make disciples of all the nations, baptizing them in the name of the Father and of the Son and of the Holy Spirit, teaching them to observe all things that I have commanded you; and lo, I am with you always, even to the end of the age.
>
> —Matthew 28:19–20

❧ Notice the steps which Jesus commands in these verses. What is involved in each?

Make Disciples:

Baptizing:

Teaching:

In what ways is Jesus with us when we share the gospel?

✎ **Today and Tomorrow** ✎

TODAY: EVERY CHRISTIAN DECLARES THE GOSPEL TO OTHERS BY OUR ACTIONS AND WORDS.

TOMORROW: I WILL ASK THE LORD TO SHOW ME HOW TO SPREAD THE GOSPEL MORE EFFECTIVELY THIS WEEK.

The Life Principles Series

Study Guides

Advancing Through Adversity
Becoming Emotionally Whole
Developing a Servant's Heart
Developing Inner Strength
Discovering Your Identity in Christ
Experiencing Forgiveness
Leaving a Godly Legacy
Listening to God
Overcoming the Enemy

Preparing for Christ's Return
Protecting Your Family
Relying on the Holy Spirit
Sharing the Gift of Encouragement
Talking with God
Understanding Eternal Security
Understanding Financial Stewardship
Winning on the Inside

Other Books by Charles Stanley

10 Principles for Studying Your Bible
Charles Stanley's Handbook For
Christian Living
Discover Your Destiny
Eternal Security
Finding Peace
The Gift of Forgiveness
How to Handle Adversity
How to Keep Your Kids on Your Team
How to Listen to God
In Step with God
Into His Presence
Landmines in the Path of the Believer

Living in the Power of the Holy Spirit
Our Unmet Needs
On Holy Ground
Pathways to His Presence
Seeking His Face
The Source of My Strength
Stuck In Reverse
Success God's Way
Walking Wisely
When the Enemy Strikes
When Your Children Hurt
Wining the War Within
The Wonderful Spirit-Filled Life